To a child who is fond of maps and engravings
The universe is the size of his immense hunger

Pour l'enfant, amoureux de cartes et d'estampes,
L'univers est égal à son vaste appétit

— Charles Baudelaire,
  from "Le Voyage," *Les Fleurs du Mal*

All works illustrated are in the collection of the Museum of Fine Arts, Houston.
Certain illustrations are covered by claims to copyright listed on page 63.

Creative direction and design: Caroline Desnoëttes
Typography and production: Ashley Edwards
Photography: Thomas R. DuBrock
Color separations, printing, and binding: Arti Grafiche Amilcare Pizzi, Italy
ISBN: 0-89090-146-5

Caroline Desnoëttes

Journeys

The Museum of Fine Arts, Houston

Welcome
to a world of art.

Let art take you on
journeys
across the continents
and the centuries.

Art can take you
anywhere
you want to go.

the traveling spirit

Pueblo (Zuni)
Doll of Mud-Head
Carrying Kiaklo Kachina
Wood, paint, wool and cotton cloth,
leather, wool yarn, gut, nails, wire,
and string; gift of Miss Ima Hogg

Frederic Remington
The Blanket Signal
Oil on canvas; the Hogg Brothers
Collection, gift of Miss Ima Hogg

Utah
c. 1896

Andy Warhol
Self-Portrait
Acrylic screenprint on canvas; gift of the Charles
Engelhard Foundation in honor of Linda L.
Cathcart, director of the Contemporary Arts
Museum from 1979 to 1987

New York
1986

Straight angles

Alabama
c. 1965

Annie Mae Young
Quilt
Cotton (shirt material, corduroy,
sheeting, etc.), polyester
(dress and pants material),
wool; museum purchase

Curving lines

Kenneth Noland
Half
Acrylic on canvas;
museum purchase

Vermont
1959

The voyage of a drop

Long Island
1949

The trace of a brush

Annie Leibovitz
Steve Martin, Beverly Hills
Silver dye bleach photograph;
The Allan Chasanoff Photographic Collection

Beverly Hills
1981

15

Soul of the country

Keith Carter
Fireflies
Gelatin silver photograph;
gift of Joan Morgenstern
in honor of Sam Lasseter

Texas
1992

Spirit of the city

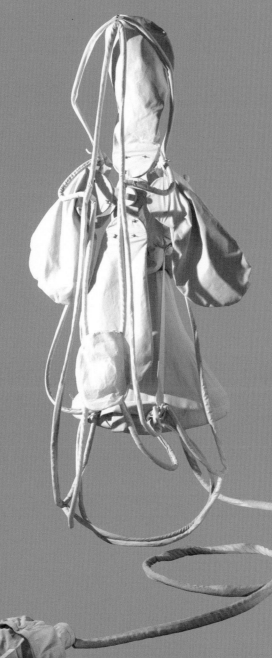

Claes Oldenburg
Giant Soft Fan,
Ghost Version
Canvas, wood, and
foam rubber; gift of
D. and J. de Menil

New York
1967

Ancient voluptuousness

Nazca
Vessel with a Caped Woman
Earthenware with polychrome slip painting;
gift of Isabel B. and Wallace S. Wilson

Peru
300–600

Modern sleekness

Francisco Matto
Totems (left to right):
Venus, Seashell, Venus, The Lamb, Mask
Venus, Seashell, Venus, and Mask are gifts of Alfred C.
Glassell III and Marli Andrade, Mary and Roy Cullen,
Marjorie H. Wortham, and Joanna and Richard W.
Wortham III; The Lamb is a gift of Ada Antuña de Matto

Uruguay
1979–85

A good laugh

Pre-Columbian,
Middle Classic Period
Seated Woman
Earthenware with traces of paint;
gift of Mrs. Harry Hanszen

Veracruz, Mexico
500–700

A happy mood

Javier Silva Meinel
La Risa
Gelatin silver photograph,
printed 2001;
gift of Mario Algaze

ancient majesty

Portrait of a Ruler
Bronze; gift of D. and J. de Menil
in memory of Conrad Schlumberger

Rome, Italy
200–225

Human and subtle

Rogier van der Weyden
Virgin and Child
Oil on wood; the Edith A. and
Percy S. Straus Collection

Netherlands
after 1454

Tender and lyrical

**Workshop of Niclaus
Weckman the Elder**
Virgin and Child
Lime wood, painted and gilded;
museum purchase with funds provided by
the Agnes Cullen Arnold Endowment Fund

Germany
c, 1500–1510

Delicate flowers

Jan van Huysum
Still Life of Flowers and Fruit
*Oil on wood; museum purchase
with funds provided by the Alice Pratt
Brown Museum Fund and the Brown
Foundation Accessions Endowment Fund*

Netherlands
c. 1715

Émile Gallé
Water Lily Vase
Glass; gift of
J. Brian and Varina Eby

France
c. 1895–1900

Impressions

Eugène Atget
Pont Marie (detail)
*Albumen printing-out-paper photograph;
gift of Lucile Bowden Johnson in honor
of Frances G. McLanahan and
Alexander K. McLanahan*

Paris, France
1926

Claude Monet
Water Lilies
Oil on canvas; gift of
Mrs. Harry C. Hanszen

Giverny, France
1907

The play of lines and colors

Pablo Picasso
Seated Woman
(Femme au grand chapeau)
Oil on canvas;
bequest of Caroline Wiess Law

France
1962

Constantin Brancusi
A Muse
Polished bronze and limestone;
gift of Mrs. Herman Brown and
Mrs. William Stamps Farish

Romania
1917

the
cradle
of humanity

Yoruba
Mother and Child Figure
Wood and traces of indigo; museum
purchase with funds provided by the
Alice Pratt Brown Museum Fund

Nigeria
late 19th century

Expressive beads

Yoruba
Crown (ade)
Glass and jasper beads, cotton cloth, raffia
cloth, cane, and iron; museum purchase with
funds provided by an anonymous donor in
honor of Anthony and Andrew Cochran

Nigeria
early 20th century

Colorful cloth

Ewe
Kente Cloth
Cotton; the Glassell Collection of
African Gold, gift of Alfred C. Glassell, Jr.

**Guinea Coast
(Ghana or Togo)**
1920–40

Golden elephants

Akan
Linguist Staff with
Elephant Finial (detail)
Wood and gold leaf; The Glassell Collection of
African Gold, gift of Alfred C. Glassell, Jr.

Ghana
19th–20th century

Akan
Crown
Wood and gold leaf; the Glassell
Collection of African Gold, gift
of Alfred C. Glassell, Jr.

Ghana
19th–20th century

Rhythm and dance

Coulibaly Siaka Paul
Dancing Man and Woman
from *Clubs of Bamako*
Polychromed wood; gift of
Nina and Michael Zilkha

Ivory Coast
1999

With the passing days

Malick Sidibé
Picnic at the Chaussée
Gelatin silver photograph,
printed 1998;
gift of Nina and Michael Zilkha

Mali
1972

Ancestral spirit

**Sala Mpasu,
Kwilu-Kasai region**
Male Helmet Mask (Idangani Society)
*Raffia, cane, other plant fibers, feathers, paint,
and twine; museum purchase with funds provided
by the Alice Pratt Brown Museum Fund*

Congo
1925–50

Ritual mask

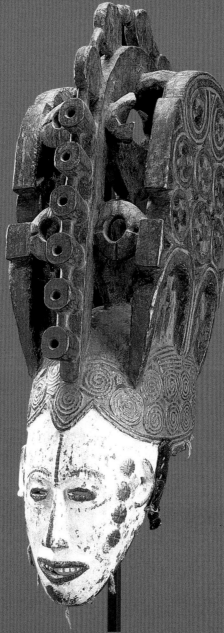

Ibo (Igbo), Mmwo society
Helmet Mask of a Maiden Spirit
Wood, kaolin, paint, wire, cotton string, and
trade cloth; museum purchase with funds
provided by the Museum Collectors

Nigeria
*Late 19th–early
20th century*

ASIA

meditative
wisdom

Klei (Unkei IX)
Amida
Wood with traces of polychrome;
museum purchase with funds provided
by the Brown Foundation Accessions
Endowment Fund

Japan
1472

43

A fan's cooling breeze

Shima Kakoku and Shima Ryu
Portrait of Shima Kakoku
Vintage negative printed as
modern albumen photograph
in 2002; museum purchase

Japan
before 1870

A refreshed feeling

幻燈寫心競

温泉

Toyohara Chikanobu
Japanese Inn at Hot Springs
Woodblock print on mulberry paper;
gift of Peter C. Knudtzon

Ando Hiroshige
View of Mountains
Woodblock print on paper;
gift of Eleanor Freed

Japan
19th century

Mountains and marvels

Osamu James Nakagawa
Mt. Fuji, Japan, Summer 1999,
from the series *Kai*
Gelatin silver photograph; gift of Joan
Morgenstern in honor of Dale Stulz

Japan
1999

Sculpted jade

Vase
*Jade (nephrite);
anonymous gift*

China
1736–96

48

Modeled clay

Tang Dynasty
Standing Court Lady
Earthenware with pigment and gold
leaf; gift of Carol and Robert Straus

China
7th century

Royal treasures

Bali, Singaraja Court
King's Necklace
Gold, rubies, sapphires, and diamonds;
the Glassell Collection of Indonesian Gold,
gift of Alfred C. Glassell, Jr.

Indonesia
late 19th century

Fit for a king

Moluccas, Luang Island
Ancestral Crown and Mask
Hammered and repoussé gold and gold
wire; the Glassell Collection of Indonesian
Gold, gift of Alfred C. Glassell, Jr.

Indonesia
17th–18th centuries

Graceful movement

Serene stillness

Madhya Pradesh
Vishnu and His Avatars
Red sandstone; museum purchase
with funds provided by the Agnes
Cullen Arnold Endowment Fund

India
c. 10th century

people
of the islands
ocean and

Western Arnhem Land
Kangaroo Painting
from a Bush Shelter
Eucalyptus bark and paint;
museum purchase

Graphic expression

**Kapriman, Middle Sepik,
Tunggambit village**
Janus-Faced Post for a Men's House
Wood, conus shell, and paint; museum purchase
with funds provided by the Director's Fund

Papua New Guinea
*first half of the
20th century*

Probably Sawos, Middle Sepik
War Shield
Wood, paint, branch, rattan, and bark; museum
purchase with funds provided by Mr. Robert
Cruikshank in honor of Mr. and Mrs. Meredith J.
Long at "One Great Night in November, 1989"

Ornamental tattoo

Asmat, Irian Jaya
War Shield (jamasj)
Wood and paint; museum purchase
with funds provided by the
Alice Pratt Brown Museum Fund

New Guinea
mid-20th century

A piercing look

Irving Penn
Tambul Warrior, New Guinea
Platinum photograph; gift of K. S. Adams, Jr.,
John S. Bace, Dr. C. Thomas Caskey, Dunbar N.
Chambers, Jr., C. Berdon Lawrence, Donald R.
Kendall, Jr., Fred Levine, Robert C. McNair,
D. Cal McNair, R. Cary McNair, and Richard C.
Walter at "One Great Night in November, 1993"

New Guinea
1970

An arresting stare

Helmet Mask (tatanua)
*Wood, paint, opercula shells,
lime plaster, plant fiber, bark,
bark cloth, rattan, and cord;
gift of an anonymous donor*

Papua New Guinea
late 19th century

Captions

Front cover and page 1: Ann Stautberg, *10-2-95, A.M., Texas Coast,* 1996, hand-colored gelatin silver photograph, partial gift of Claude and Susan Albritton, Andre and Sylvia Crispin, Joan Morgenstern, and Clinton T. Willour.

Back cover, page 3, and throughout: Joel Shapiro, *Untitled,* 1990, bronze, edition 4/4, gift of Isabell and Max Herzstein in memory of Benjamin K. Smith.

Pages 5 and 61: James Turrell, *The Light Inside,* 1999, neon light, projected light, gypsum board, plaster, glass, and oak, museum commission with funds provided by Isabel B. and Wallace S. Wilson.

Page 6: Dennis Blagg, *Nugent Mountain* (detail), 1993, oil on canvas, gift of William R. Camp, Jr., in honor of Frank J. Hevrdejs and Louis Tenenbaum at "One Great Night in November, 1993."

Page 7: Frederick Judd Waugh, *Mid Ocean* (detail), oil on canvas, gift of Mrs. William Stamps Farish.

Page 60: Robert Frank, *U.S. 285, New Mexico,* from the series *The Americans,* 1955, gelatin silver photograph, printed 1977, gift of Jerry E. and Nanette Finger.

Credits

Work by Eugène Atget © Estate of Eugène Atget

Work by Constantin Brancusi © 2007 Artists Rights Society (ARS), New York/ADAGP, Paris

Work by Dennis Blagg © Dennis Blagg

Work by Keith Carter © Keith Carter

Work by Robert Frank © Robert Frank, courtesy of PaceWildenstein MacGill

Work by Annie Leibovitz © Annie Leibovitz

Work by Francisco Matto © Estate of Francisco Matto

Work by Javier Silva Meinel © Javier Silva Meinel

Work by Osamu James Nakagawa © Osamu James Nakagawa

Work by Kenneth Noland © Kenneth Noland/Licensed by VAGA, New York, NY

Work by Claes Oldenburg © Claes Oldenburg

Work by Coulibaly Siaka Paul © Coulibaly Siaka Paul

Work by Irving Penn © Irving Penn

Work by Pablo Picasso © 2007 Estate of Pablo Picasso/Artists Rights Society (ARS), New York

Work by Jackson Pollock © 2007 Pollock-Krasner Foundation/Artists Rights Society (ARS), New York

Work by Joel Shapiro © 2007 Joel Shapiro/Artists Rights Society (ARS), New York

Work by Malick Sibidé © Malick Sibidé

Work by James Turrell © James Turrell; photographs © by Mike Stude

Work by Andy Warhol © 2007 Andy Warhol Foundation for the Visual Arts/ Artists Rights Society (ARS), New York

Work by Annie Mae Young © Annie Mae Young

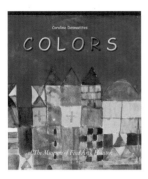

About the Author

Caroline Desnoëttes is a painter, designer, and author of books for children and adults, including *Colors of the Museum of Fine Arts, Houston*. She lives in France.